THE ART OF HAIR COLOURING

David Adams and Jacki Wadeson

THOMSON

HABIA

City & Guilds

The Art Of Hair Colouring

The Thomson logo is a registered trademark used herein under licence.

For more information, contact Thomson Learning, High Holborn House, 50-51 Bedford Row, London WC1R 4LR or visit us on the World Wide Web at:
http://www.thomsonlearning.co.uk

British Library Cataloguing-in-Publication Data
A catalogue record for this book is available from the British Library

First published in 1998 by Macmillan Press Ltd

This version printed 2002 by Thomson Learning
Reprinted 2004 and 2005 (twice) by Thomson Learning

ISBN-13: 978-1-86152-894-0
ISBN-10: 1-86152-894-9

Printed in Croatia by Zrinski

Using 'he or she' and 'him or her' throughout the text would become cumbersome in a book such as this. For simplicity and ease of reading, therefore, we have used simply 'she' and 'her' throughout.

Books by Jacki Wadeson:
Hairstyle file
Braiding
Braiding fun
Hairstyles, braiding & haircare
My braiding book
Patrick Cameron: Dressing Long Hair

Contents

ACKNOWLEDGEMENTS

Hair colour: *David Adams*
Assisted by: *Margarita Blanco*
Colour: *Belavance Color by Labothene International,*
Pforzheim, Germany
Equipment and utensils: *Comby Ltd, Matador combs and gloves,*
and Pro-Tip brushes
Cutting: *Stephane Gallien*
Styling: *Kylie Compton*
Make-up: *Teresa Fairminer*
Still life: *Barry Cook*
Photography: *Alistair Hughes*
Assisted by: *Neil Geugan*
Editor: *Jacki Wadeson*

With thanks to Pat Dixon, Katrina Garner, George Hammer
and Andrew Wilson.

Stephane Gallien, David Adams, Kylie Compton and Margarita Blanco
from the Urban Retreat Salon in Harvey Nichols, and make-up artist
Teresa Fairminer.

With special thanks to Mr Siegfried Weiser
of Labothene International, Pforzheim, Germany,
without whom this book would not have been possible.

Hairdressing Training Board/Thomson Series

Start Hairdressing! – The Official Guide to Level 1
By Martin Green & Leo Palladino ISBN 1-861-52681-4

Hairdressing: The Foundations – The Official Guide to Level 2
By Leo Palladino ISBN 1-861-52671-7

Professional Hairdressing – The Official Guide to Level 3
By Leo Palladino ISBN 1-861-52661-X

Patrick Cameron: Dressing Long Hair
By Patrick Cameron & Jacki Wadeson ISBN 1-861-52701-2

Mahogany: Steps to Cutting, Colouring and Finishing Hair
By Martin Gannon & Richard Thompson ISBN 1-861-52693-8

African-Caribbean Hairdressing
By Sandra Gittens ISBN 1-861-52695-4

Safety in the Salon: A Guide for Hairdressing and Beauty Professionals
By Elaine Almond ISBN 0-333-73006-2

The Art of Hair Colouring
By David Adams & Jacki Wadeson ISBN 1-861-52894-9

Trevor Sorbie: Visions in Hair
By Trevor Sorbie ISBN 0-333-74714-3

FOREWORD

I'm a dreamweaver, what's more, when I weave I do it in colour. If I have to create a new product or develop an idea I need to do this when I'm most relaxed and this is what I call dreamweaving. I picture ideas in my mind and look at the processes that need to be undertaken to achieve the desired effect. I need to see everything in colour and everything in its perspective. This book does just that too. It weaves the impossible balance between product information and brilliant creative work. The simplicity of Jacki Wadeson's writing is matched by David Adams' considerable and highly sought after skill in pushing colouring hair to its limits. This book should be read by hairdressers who want to express themselves in colour.

Alan Goldsbro

Chief Executive
Hairdressing Training Board

PREFACE

Colour is the finishing touch to every haircut – it brings hair alive and gives depth, texture and tone. Gone are the days when it was simply used to mask grey. Today colour echoes the changing fashion and cosmetic moods of our ever-evolving fashion scene.

All colourists need to have at their fingertips a cornucopia of techniques that allow them to re-invent their clients on a regular basis. Whilst highlights and whole head tints will always be popular, more and more clients have lost their shyness about colour and want bolder, stronger looks that make a statement.

In our book we take you through the history, psychology and science of colour. We explain the basics and combine them with the artistic to show you how your creativity can be enhanced by your skill and the depth of your own imagination.

David Adams and Jacki Wadeson

HISTORY

Since time immemorial all manner of plants, potions and lotions have been used to change the colour of hair. Cleopatra was said to have anointed her hair with henna before bathing in the Nile. To lighten their hair, Roman women used pungent concoctions of wood ash, unslaked lime and sodium bicarbonate. For darker hues they opted for a mixture of copper filings and oak-apples. Also favoured was a hair blackening liquid made from leeches which had been left to putrefy for 60 days in an earthenware pot with wine and vinegar. At the thermal springs in Wiesbaden, Germany, the Teutons mixed lead oxide, ochre and vermilion with soap to form a substance called 'Sapo' which they used to cleanse and colour the hair red.

After the collapse of the Roman Empire, beauty secrets spread eastwards to Constantinople. Here, Turkish women used finely pulverised fruit of the gall-oak, kneaded with oil and blended with white lead, to form a blackening paste.

During the Renaissance women bleached their hair with a mixture of borax and saltpetre or a liquid solution produced by boiling water, lupins, gorse, saffron, gelatine, mullein and exotic myrrh. To obtain titian hues they spread their hair on the brims of crownless hats and applied a paste of ashes and herbs. By sitting in the sun the ladies could acquire red and copper tones.

In the fifteenth century formulas for bleached hair were guarded jealously but history tells us that recipes contained lizard fat, swallows' droppings and the ashes of bears' bones. Saffron, sulphur, alum and honey were also used. These recipes were not always safe and in 1562 a certain Dr Marinello from Modena in Italy wrote a treatise warning of the possible and undesirable consequences of bleaches: 'The scalp could be seriously damaged and the hair be destroyed at the roots and fall out.'

It wasn't until the early nineteenth century that hydrogen peroxide was discovered. It was first used in 1860 by Napoleon II's mistress, Cora Pearl.

In 1859 a German professor, Wilhelm Hofman of London's Royal College of Chemistry, was researching coal-tar derivatives. One of his students, William Henry Perk, was attempting to synthesise quinine and ended up with a black sludge. Rather than give up, he diluted the sludge with alcohol and it turned purple. This discovery led to the creation of permanent dyes that could be used on fabric and hair and it eventually led to the development of the synthetic hair colourants we use today.

Psychology

Colour surrounds us constantly, even in our dreams. When we see the changing sky, the brilliance of the sun, the hues of the natural world, it is difficult to imagine a world without colour. It fills our bodies, interacts with our energies and affects our moods, making things appear warm or cold, provocative or sympathetic, exciting or tranquil.

Our perception of time is affected by colour. Kurt Goldstein, a neuropsychologist who experimented with coloured illumination, concluded that in red light, time is overestimated and objects seem longer, bigger or heavier; while in green or blue light, time is underestimated and objects seem shorter, smaller and lighter.

The healing properties of colour have been appreciated since the beginning of time. They were part of the ancient wisdom taught and practised in the great temples of Egypt and Greece, in China, India and Tibet. They were also part of the Mayan culture of Central America and the tribal lore of the North American Indians.

Children given yellow and brown crayons to illustrate happy and sad stories will instinctively choose yellow for the happy pictures and brown for the sad ones. Wards in psychiatric hospitals are painted blue as it has a calming effect on the patients. Yellow is never used in aircraft because it can induce nausea, but it is applied to classroom walls to improve the work of schoolchildren.

When we use colours to describe people and emotions, e.g. 'green with envy', 'purple with rage', 'cowardly yellow' or 'seeing red', we are expressing common associations that may have more truth than we realise. Throughout our lives we use colour as a cue for interpreting what we see, and this applies to hair colours too.

Blondes, redheads and brunettes are all imbued with behavioural and stereotyped images whose very roots are steeped in antiquity. Psychologists say that the reason we accept these stereotyped images is that human nature abhors chaos and the mind tends to latch onto a single powerful cue and embellish it with all sorts of associations from the past. Robert Scott, a sociologist at the Centre for Advanced Study in Behavioural Sciences in Palo Alto, California, says that instant categorisation, based on the colour of a person's hair, can act as a social lubricant. It gives us the impression that we know something about a person before we even speak to them.

THE COLOUR WE SEE

It was Sir Isaac Newton who, in the seventeenth century, discovered that the white light from the sun contains all the colours one can see. He proved his theory by allowing a beam of light to pass through a glass prism. The light waves were bent at different angles to create a fan-shaped pattern. The colours are always arranged in the same order: red, orange, yellow, green, blue, indigo and violet – the colours of the rainbow.

When we look at an object, what we actually see is light reflected from it. A white object reflects most of the white light that falls on it; a black object absorbs most of the light falling on it; a red object reflects red light and absorbs everything else; a blue object reflects the blue light and absorbs everything else, and so on.

Hair colour depends chiefly on the pigments in the hair which absorb some of the light and reflect the rest. The colour we see is also affected by the light in which we see it and, to a lesser extent, by the colours of clothes and make-up worn with it.

Blondes

Blonde hair has always been coveted. Around AD 500, if a person was not naturally blonde, they would spare no expense in endeavouring to attain the golden shade that was thought to characterise 'children of the God of Light'. In the Middle Ages, anyone without blonde hair was thought to lack status and character or to hail from a barbarian nation. To the Anglo Saxons, 'fair' meant handsome and free-born, while 'dark' was the colour of the conquering Celts, the 'ugly' colouring of the enslaved.

Early this century, going for gold was a risky commitment. Jean Harlow's famous platinum blonde hair broke off because every week she anointed it with a mixture of hydrogen peroxide, household bleach, soap flakes and ammonia. This probably explains why she wore wigs from the age of 24 until her death at 26. Hollywood has always had its share of blonde goddesses but the archetypal blonde is surely Marilyn Monroe. She picked up the hydrogen peroxide bottle and created a cult look which was copied by Jayne Mansfield, Diana Dors and – more recently – Madonna, but no one else has quite mirrored her image.

Cool blondeness was personified by Grace Kelly in the 1950s, dizziness by Barbara Windsor in the Carry On films of the 1960s and 1970s, and innocence and fragility by Twiggy in the 1960s. In the 1980s Debbie Harry and her platinum locks and spray-on micro-skirt hit the charts with her band Blondie. She never tried to hide the fact that her hair was lightened – she even boasted dark roots on her record sleeves and she created the grunge blonde look. Perhaps the most powerful blonde of the century was the Iron Lady herself, Margaret Thatcher, whose hair lightened as her years in office increased.

STEREOTYPES

The debate about whether 'gentlemen prefer blondes' has raged since the release of the film with that title in 1953. It is also often said that blondes have more fun, but this could simply be because we tend to notice them more.

COLOURING

Northern European hair that is naturally blonde in childhood often dulls off in later life and becomes 'mouse-coloured'. This is the perfect natural base for lightening because the skin tone and eye colour will be perfect. There are many nuances of blonde, ranging from cool nordic through subtle warm strawberry shades to brilliant gold tones. Blonde hair is much easier to make lighter than any other colour. When darkening it you must put a base in with the colour to stabilise it.

Blonde hair is adaptable to any colouring process. However, you have to bear in mind hair texture, natural lightness, skin tone and eye colour and the amount of white hair, if any. With blue eyes, black looks wonderful. If the eyes are green, red is a stunning choice.

PROBLEMS

The staining caused by nicotine from cigarette smoke and by chemicals in swimming pools affects all hair colours. Unfortunately, it tends to show more on blondes. Nicotine staining can be disguised by using blue-toned rinses or colour shampoos. Clients who swim regularly should be advised to rinse their hair thoroughly after swimming and use chelating shampoos that remove mineral, chlorine and chemical build-up from the hair shaft.

Blondes are said to have more fun

REDHEADS

Red hair has always symbolised blood-lust and bad luck. The Ancient Greeks decreed that red hair was taboo and that all strangers, rogues and the red-headed should be treated with contempt. In the early Middle Ages, antipathy was still felt against those with red hair: 'Trust no redhead, for these are wicked and ill-tempered people', was the warning contained in the epic poem 'Ruodlieb' written in AD 1000. A red-haired person such as Otto II, Holy Roman Emperor 973–983, was accordingly regarded as a bad lot. For the same reason, in works of art from about 1300 onwards the traitor Judas was portrayed with red hair. In the fifteenth century red-haired women ran the risk of being denounced as witches.

Elizabeth I (1533–1603) was responsible for changing the bad press of redheads: her natural titian tresses suddenly made red hair fashionable. At the same time, the spirit and passion of Shakespeare's vibrant heroines was personified by red hair.

This century, Hollywood movies helped promote a brand-new glamourous image for redheads, with colourful actresses such as Rita Hayworth, Deborah Kerr and sexy Ann-Margaret becoming box-office hits. On TV in the 1950s, Lucille Ball added comedy to the carrot-top repertoire, and in 1981 *Thelma and Louise* first combined feminism, violence and red hair on the big screen. More recently, Sharon Stone, Emily Lloyd and Kylie Minogue have all flirted with titian tresses.

STEREOTYPES

With so much bad press over the years it's no wonder that red hair brings to mind fieriness. The Duchess of York is repeatedly criticised for being headstrong and impetuous – and some suggest that we should expect nothing less from a flame-haired woman. It was also said that the colour of Neil Kinnock's hair was partly responsible for his failure to win a general election – people didn't trust him.

COLOURING

Certain products are specially suited for use on redheads, and while all types can be used, vegetable colour gives good results, enhancing the gloss and tone. To make highlights work, you need a strong contrast, and the classic choice is the stronger reds or crimson. Alternatively, try light and dark browns – anything in the middle tends to look wrong. If opting for browns, chestnut tones darken but retain the warmth. Flying colours (see p. 111) that are 'painted on' are ideal as they give the impression of movement to the hair, especially with shorter styles. Another good alternative is to use multi-toned reds running throughout.

The most common complaint from red-haired clients after a colouring service is that the colour isn't strong enough and they can't see any difference, so be bold. However, keep in mind that your colour choice must complement the pale complexion and eye colour.

Lightening a whole head can be more difficult, especially if you want to go from dark red to cool blonde. As the hair lightens, it is usually difficult to get it past a pale orange, which then needs to be corrected.

PROBLEMS

Red tones are particularly prone to fade because the colour molecules are larger than any other and can escape more easily. Clients should be advised to protect their hair from the sun and rinse away salt and chlorine. Specialist shampoos and conditioners for coloured hair will help maintain the colour. However, advise clients against the use of colour refreshers if the hair has been bleached. Such products can 'grab' onto lighter sections and give a piebald effect.

Redheads are thought to be impulsive and reckless

BRUNETTES

Brunette hair was so prized in Egyptian times that doctors mixed up the most obnoxious potions to prevent greyness. The blood of a black calf, a bullock and a snake were combined with oil and rubbed into the scalp. If this failed, bitumen and stibium were used to darken hair. In Greek mythology, the power of Medea, the sorceress who fell in love with Jason, leader of the Argonauts, depended on her skill as a perfumer and her ability to use vegetable dye to turn grey hair black. In the seventeenth century, grated nutmeg was sprinkled onto wigs to make them look darker. In 1772 it was George Washington who abandoned his wig, displayed his brown locks and set a trend for plain hair and even plainer speaking.

STEREOTYPES

Brunettes tend to be regarded as approachable, natural, open and – sometimes – just plain. Perhaps our most famous and internationally loved brunette was Audrey Hepburn, who, as the archetypal coquette in *Breakfast at Tiffany's*, became a role model for a generation of girls in the 1950s.

Princess Caroline of Monaco is an example of a classic brunette. While Cindy Crawford has made millions out of her brown hair by adding a blonde Dynasty streak to the front section.

Others have tried to capture the look and those who have flirted with burnished hues include Annie Lennox, Paula Yates and Bridget Neilson.

COLOURING

Brown hair is very often thick, healthy and glossy, and people blessed with this colour often have a beautiful skin tone to complement it. Any type of colour can be used on brown hair and the results are excellent. However, you must remember that you are adding colour to a darker base, so bear this in mind when making your selection.

When lightening, remember that the natural pigments are going to come out of the hair shaft in this order: red, red/orange, orange, so unexpected warmth may be experienced. Also, when you add colour to brunettes, because of the intensity of depth (see below), the colour may strengthen and appear darker than required. So always veer to the lighter shades in order to compensate for this.

It is very difficult to assess pigmentation just by looking at the hair, so always test an underneath section using a totally neutral base colour. The lightest base you should consider using is probably a 6 depth, i.e. dark blonde. The depth of brown should also be considered in relation to the skin tone. With brunettes it is often best to go lighter rather than darker, by a few shades.

On Indian hair, chestnut and caramel tonal lights look good, giving the client the opportunity to look special and different. Adding warmth and richness can work very well, too.

With brunettes it is best to customise colours and techniques that suit the individual client. When doing highlights, use soft blondes and lighter golds.

PROBLEMS

Be careful when using a 4 depth because on fine hair around the hairline it can intensify dramatically and give a very hard, dark result. Finally, taking brown hair too light can sometimes give a 'dirty' look due to the incompatibility of hair and skin tone.

GOING GREY

As we age, melanin production slows down and colourless or white hairs begin to appear. These hairs mix with darker ones on the head and give the impression of grey. At 35 most people have some white hair and by the age of 50 more than half the population have at least 50 per cent grey.

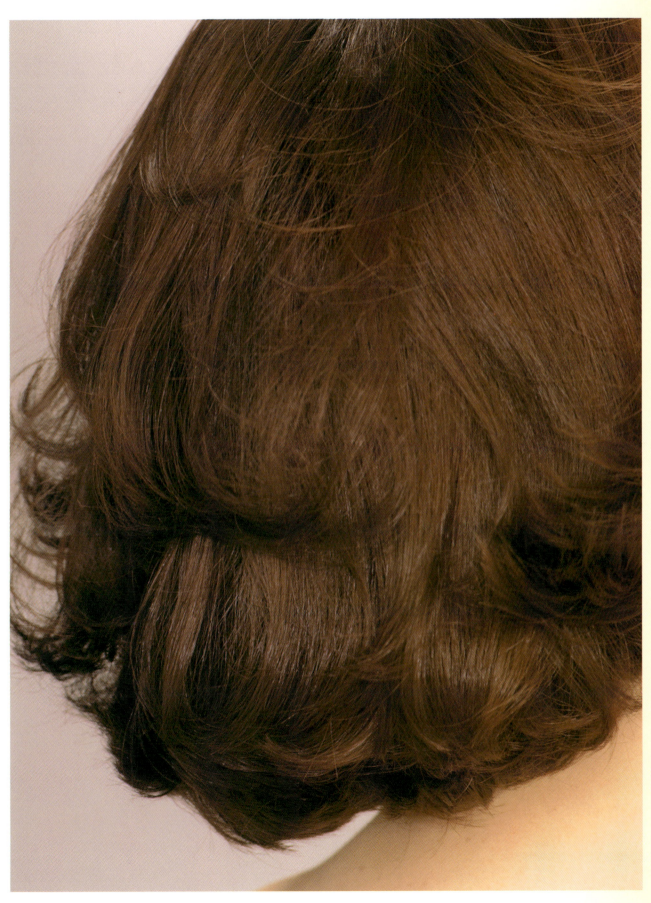

Brunettes are instinctively associated with warmth and cheer

Whatis colour?

NATURAL PIGMENTATION

Colour is formed in the cortex of the hair by melanocytes which produce two types of pigment: melanins, which are black/brown, and pheomelanins, which are red/yellow. All natural hair colours are a combination of these two types of pigment. Dark-haired people have more black/brown pigments while the fairer-skinned nationalities have more red/yellow pigment. It is the variation in these pigments that produces the spectrum of different hair colours.

THE COLOUR CIRCLE

The laws of colour regulate the mixing of dyes and pigments to create other colours. The first concept of these laws is basic hue. Hues are arranged around the colour circle in a manner that shows the relationship among colours. The circle is divided into four categories: primary, secondary, tertiary and quarternary.

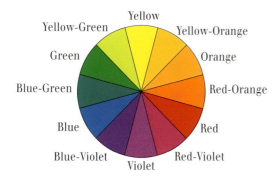

The **primary** colours are red, yellow and blue. These pure colours cannot be made by mixing other colours together.

Secondary colours combine two primary colours, e.g.:
yellow + red = orange   blue + yellow = green
red + blue = violet

Tertiary colours are created by combining equal amounts of adjacent primary and secondary colours, e.g.:
red – orange   yellow – green   blue – violet
yellow – orange   blue – green   red – violet

Quarternary colours are all the other combinations of colour, including all the colours the eye can see.

NEUTRALISING EFFECT OF COLOURS

According to the laws of colour, if you mix equal proportions of the hues that are positioned directly across from each other on the colour circle, they will neutralise each other, e.g. green neutralises red, orange neutralises blue, violet neutralises yellow, and vice versa.

Knowing which colour neutralises which is a vital part of a colourist's work because it facilitates the removal of unwanted tones from the hair.

DESCRIBING NATURAL COLOUR

The terms depth and tone are used to describe natural colour. **Depth** is an indication of how light or dark the colour is, and this depends on the intensity of the pigments within the hair. **Tone** is the colour you see, i.e. the combination of the pigments. Warm shades such as gold or red have more red/yellow pigments. Cool shades such as ash have fewer.

ICS

ICS, the International Colouring System, offers a system of defining hair colours. Shades are divided and numbered like this:

Depth		Tone	
1/0	blue-black	/0	natural
2/0	black	/1	ash
3/0	dark brown	/2	cool ash
4/0	medium brown	/3	honey gold
5/0	light brown	/4	red
6/0	dark blonde	/5	purple
7/0	medium blonde	/6	violet
8/0	light blonde	/7	brunette
9/0	very light blonde	/8	pearl ash
10/0	extra light blonde	/9	soft ash

Therefore a colour which has the number 6/1 is the depth of dark blonde with ash tones, so it will be dark ash blonde.

CONSULTATION

Every prospective colour client should be encouraged to come into the salon for a consultation before their appointment. This is time well spent as it gives the colourist an opportunity to assess the client's personality, lifestyle, hair type and image expectations.

Most colour problems are due to a lack of communication between colourist and client, so it is important not to rush the consultation – allow at least half an hour. Taking the time to do a strand test and a skin test may well save you problems later on.

When the client comes into the salon, invite her to sit down in front of your workstation and introduce yourself – you'd be surprised how many stylists forget basic courtesy. Rather than covering her up with a gown, take the opportunity to assess her character from the clothes she is wearing. Ask her about her lifestyle and what type of image she wants to project. Ask her about her hair colour, what colours she has tried in the past and whether she liked the result. Listen intently to what she tells you. Find out why she wants to colour her hair. Is it to cover grey? To get a sunlifted effect? Does she want a discreet or drastic change? What colours does she like or dislike? What sort of commitment to colour is she prepared to make? It is also important to assess her mood: if she is nervous, explanations may take longer; if she is excited, she may may be willing to go for a more drastic change.

Next, look at her hair and ascertain if it already has a colour, whether it is professional or retail, and see if the hair has been permed or relaxed. Check the client's skin tone and eye colour. Your choice of colour must complement both, and add warmth to the skin tone. Run your fingers through her hair to examine any previous colour applications and check the scalp for irritations or skin problems.

The most important question to ask yourself is 'Can I colour this hair and keep it in good condition?' Never promise anything you can't deliver. At this stage introduce your client to the person who will be cutting her hair. It is important that colour and cut are designed to work together.

Once you know what she has in mind, you can begin to formulate your ideas. People's perception of colour differs, so at this stage it is a good idea to look at some pictures. Many salons compile books of magazine cuttings that show different hair colours and styles. Don't show a client a manufacturer's shade chart as these may cause confusion.

Armed with the results of your analysis of the client and the answers to your questions, it is a good idea to suggest three colouring options – soft, medium and strong – explaining each in detail. Unless you are completely sure of your client, it is normally best to start with a soft and gentle colour that you know she will be happy with. Once you have gained your client's confidence, you can progress to to something bolder on subsequent visits. If your client insists on having something you are not happy with, you must be firm and stand your ground. Explain why this option won't work and try to steer her in another direction.

Once you have both reached a decision, you must double check that you can achieve what the client wants. Before proceeding you must do strand and skin tests, which are explained opposite. Once the tests have been completed successfully, you should summarise the colour you intend to apply and what the result will be. Explain about upkeep of the colour, how long each salon visit will take and how much it will cost. If the colour change is quite drastic, you may have to advise your client to adjust her make-up colours and perhaps re-assess her wardrobe.

HOW TO DO A STRAND TEST

A strand test enables you to monitor colour development and avoid potential problems caused by previous colour applications. The procedure is similar for regrowth tints and for full head colouring. It is normal to do a strand test on or just under the crown but occasionally other parts of the head will be more appropriate. Take a strand of hair and apply the tint you are planning to use. Wrap the strand in foil and allow the product to develop. Remove with damp cotton wool and look to see if the colour has developed evenly. If you are doing a strand test for a regrowth application, the tint should be applied to the roots only. The developed colour of the roots can then be compared with that of the lengths and ends.

HOW TO DO A SKIN TEST

Cleanse a small area of skin either behind the ear or on the inside of the elbow using surgical spirit on cotton wool. Mix a small amount of tint and the hydrogen peroxide you intend to use and apply to the cleansed area. Allow to dry and cover the area with collodion, which will leave a clear film over it. Advise the client to leave the patch alone and return to the salon the next day to see if there is a reaction. If there is any irritation, however slight, under no circumstances should any other chemical hair colour be applied to the hair.

Client consultation is one of the most important points of hair colouring.

EQUIPMENT

Your choice of accessories can give a vibrant edge to your work, so it is worth taking a little time when choosing which to buy and use in the salon.

BOWLS

Use strong plastic bowls or the new ceramic ones. Avoid those with metal edges to avoid the risk of adverse reactions between the metal and the chemicals. There are often marked measurement levels on the inside of the bowl to ensure accuracy. Such bowls can be used for all colouring purposes. Opt for ones with a heavy base as lightweight bowls can tip over easily. Some bases are covered or edged with rubber to prevent slipping and these are a practical design to choose.

BRUSHES AND SPONGES

Brushes are usually made of hardened rubber or plastic and have square, flat bristles at one end. The other end of the brush is usually pointed so that sectioning and application can be carried out with one tool. Choose large or small to suit the application technique. Generally, colour is mixed and applied with the same brush.

Sponges are made of foam. They have one serrated edge and one flat edge that fits into a plastic grip.

CLIPS

Available in a variety of colours and styles, clips are used when sectioning the hair. Metal clips can be used provided they do not come into contact with chemicals. Crocodile clips are good for keeping long hair out of the way while you are working on lower sections.

COLOUR DISPENSERS AND MEASURES

Applicator bottles are essential for accurate measuring and to ensure even application of chemicals that are too runny to apply by the bowl/brush method. Choose bottles in high quality plastic with clear markings and efficient nozzles.

Plastic measures with measuring guides embossed on the outside are the most practical for decanting colour.

COMBS

Hard rubber combs better known as ebonite or vulcanite are mainly a mixture of natural and synthetic rubber developed especially for products calling for elasticity and workability. Many experts believe that vulcanite surpasses all plastics and metal for the art of comb making. It is essential that combs used on clients are anti-static, precision made and have saw cut teeth so they won't drag or tear the hair. Every colourist's kit bag should include a variety of combs from pintail to large style designs.

FOILS

Aluminium foil comes in rolls which can be cut to the size required. Different coloured foils add a certain finesse to your colour work and may provide a key for colour placement.

HAND AND SKIN PROTECTION

Gloves are available in various sizes and thicknesses. They are made of plastic, polythene or fine rubber and should be used to protect your hands during all technical services. It is essential to take extra care to protect your hands – they are your most important asset. Cotton wool strips and barrier cream are also essential to protect clients' skin from staining.

PROTECTIVE APRONS, SHOULDER WRAPS

It makes sense to protect the clothing of your staff and your clients from staining and damage caused by chemicals. Many clients prefer to remove jackets and tops prior to a colouring service and wear gowns provided by the salon. Disposable polythene aprons and wraps for the colourist also reduce the laundry bills.

RECORD CARDS

These are vital. They should be filled in after every client visit and stored in alphabetical order in a filing box. Make a note of exactly what was used, by whom and at what cost.

Name ....
Address ....
.... Postcode ....
Daytime telephone number ....
Date ....
Stylist ....
Scalp condition ....
Hair type ....
Technique ....
Products used ....
Development time ....
Result achieved ....
Removal / after care ....
Price charged ....
Special comments ....
....
....

VEGETABLE DYES

True vegetable dyes are derived from herbs, plants, flowers, vegetables, minerals and the bark of trees. They are made into infusions and pastes and will enhance colour and can add an incredible gloss and shine.

HOW TO MAKE AN INFUSION

The basic recipe is 2 x 25 ml (2 tablespoons) of fresh herbs, leaves and/or flowers to 600 ml (1 pint) of boiling water. (With dried herbs use half the quantity as they are stronger than fresh ones.) Pour water over and leave to steep for at least 15 minutes, but ideally for up to 3 hours. The longer the infusion steeps, the stronger the properties of the rinse. Use a glass or china container and keep the brew covered while it is infusing. After steeping, strain the liquid before use.

Camomile contains a yellow colourant which, when infused and used as a final rinse on mousey or lighter hair, will give a lightening effect. Alternatively, a paste can be made using 2 tablespoons of dried flower-heads crushed with 2 tablespoons of kaolin. Mix with water to form a smooth paste and apply as for henna (see p. 18).

Rhubarb root will lighten brown bases and give golden highlights if the application is followed by a spell in the sun. Boil a handful of rhubarb roots in water for an hour, cool and strain the liquid, then use as a final rinse. Rhubarb root is not suitable for use on blonde or white hair as it can leave a yellowish tinge.

Saffron gives bright yellow hues to natural blonde, tinted or bleached hair. First boil a few strands of saffron in 1 pint of water, then dilute the liquid to the strength required before using it as a water rinse.

Marigold gives a weak yellow tinge and an infusion of flowers can be used as a final rinse to soften lighter bases.

Sage darkens the hair and an infusion is generally used on grey hair to take away whiter elements and tone the colour to a more silvery slate.

Cascarilla is a tree bark that yields a strong black dye which can be used to give brown tones to grey hair. The bark should be infused, cooled and used as a final rinse.

Walnuts can be used to darken hair. To make the dye, boil the shells in water for two hours, strain and cool the liquid and use it as a final rinse.

Quassia is a tree bark that is often used with camomile to produce a colourant which brightens the hair.

Other substances such as sumach, oak bark, cudbear and logwood are sometimes used to produce various shades and effects, to give natural colouring results.

ADVANTAGES
- no skin tests required
- natural products
- dyes coat rather than enter the hair shaft

DISADVANTAGES
- dyes do not cover white hair
- applications must be regular to maintain the colour

TIP

Vegetable infusions and dyes must only be used on virgin hair, never over any other chemical colours. Results can vary depending on the quality of the natural ingredients used and the porosity of the hair.

Henna

Used to add colour and shine to hair throughout history, henna is a gentle colouring option. It comes from the dried leaves of the privet *Lawsonia alba* that grows in Asia and northern Africa. The active ingredient is lawsone, which was first isolated in 1709 by the famous botanist Dr Israel Lawson. It has conditioning and colouring properties that have been used as a beauty aid in Europe since 1890.

The leaves are harvested, dried in the sun and then crushed into a green powder. If the leaves are collected before they are fully mature, the product is known as green henna, which produces a more delicate shade of red with a slight yellow tone. Fully mature henna produces a richer red. Indigo is sometimes mixed with henna to produce Persian henna, which dyes the hair blue-black. Other variants are the result of mixing henna with herbs such as camomile or sage.

Neutral henna comes from the crushed root of the plant and is used for conditioning rather than colouring.

Henna is a coating dye, which means that it stains the cuticle or outer layer of the hair. The degree of staining depends on the natural colour and porosity of the hair. Long hair, because it has been exposed to the sun over a period of time, will show a tonal variation along the length when henna is used. Colour fades gradually, so regular applications (every six to eight weeks) are needed to keep the intensity of tone. When henna is applied to brunette or black hair, you get a warm, reddish glow, while lighter hair goes a reddish gold. You can't lighten hair with henna and it is not suitable for use on hair that is white, tinted, bleached or highlighted. The result varies according to the length of time the henna is left on the hair. Some Indian women leave henna on their hair for up to 24 hours, anointing their heads with oil to keep the paste supple.

COMPOUND HENNA

Natural henna is sometimes mixed with a compound containing metallic salts to produce a full range of colours. Popular in Western Europe, compound henna makes the hair unsuitable for future treatment with any product that includes hydrogen peroxide. If your client is not sure what type of henna has been used on her hair, it is essential that you do a strand test to check for metallic deposits before you undertake any other chemical process. Previous use of compound henna on the hair will show up in the strand test as:

• strong discolouration

• an unpleasant odour

• no colour change whatsoever

• uneven colour result down length of strand

HOW TO USE

Natural henna is normally mixed to a smooth paste with hot water or with milk, which gives a creamier, easier to apply consistency. At this stage other ingredients can be added that intensify or change the tone. Red wine gives a deeper tone, while the addition of coffee results in a beautiful chestnut brown that is especially good on greying hair. The paste should be applied with a brush from the roots to the ends of shampooed and towel-dried hair, coiling each section out of the way once it has been treated. Henna is messy and will stain the skin and nails so it is essential for the colourist to wear gloves and protective clothing and to smear a barrier cream round the client's hairline and ears. Covering the hair with a foil will trap in heat and intensify the result. After the required time, hair should be rinsed and then shampooed two or three times to remove any remaining particles of colour. (For step-by-step application instructions, see pp. 20–22.)

BENEFITS

One of the best things about henna is that it is non-toxic, non-irritating and adds shine and body to the hair, as well as a range of subtle, reddish hues. Subsequent applications deposit additional protective coatings, which can make fine hair appear temporarily thicker. Henna sometimes helps to clear up dandruff.

Neutral henna can be used to add gloss and lustre. To do this, mix henna to a stiff paste with water and, for extra conditioning, stir in an egg yolk and a little milk. Apply and leave for an hour before rinsing thoroughly. This should be repeated every two to three months.

DISADVANTAGES

Henna can dry the hair and continued use can lead to harsh colour. The only way to get rid of henna is to allow it to grow out. Problems can arise with hair treatments such as perms and chemical colours if a client who has used henna in the past assumes that because the colour has faded the hair is back to its natural state. It is essential to do a strand test (see p.13) so that you can ascertain what type of henna has been used and whether or not subsequent chemical treatments are advisable.

HOW TO APPLY HENNA

Before

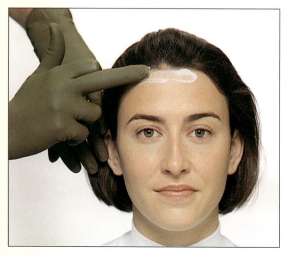

1 Apply barrier cream around the hairline.

2 Take a section from the crown down to the nape of the neck. Apply the henna to the root area only.

3 Take the next section from the crown down to the top of the ear, and apply the henna.

TIPS

- Always do a strand test before using henna.

- Shampoo hair thoroughly before application.

- Advise clients not to expose hennaed hair to strong sunlight.

- Hennaed hair should be rinsed thoroughly after swimming.

- Henna application can be repeated every two to three months.

TIP

Remember to cross-check root application, i.e. take sections the opposite way to check that no area has been missed.

4 Take diagonal sections across the back of the head and apply the henna.

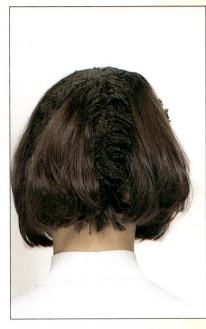

5 Completed root application at the back.

6 Now take diagonal sections across the front and apply the henna to the roots.

7 Completed root application from the front.

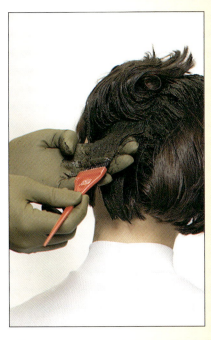

8 Starting at the nape of the neck, apply the henna to the mid-lengths and ends.

9 To ensure completely even coverage, massage the henna into the hair and mould it into a top-knot.

10 Re-apply the barrier cream around the hairline, then place a strip of cotton wool on top of the cream.

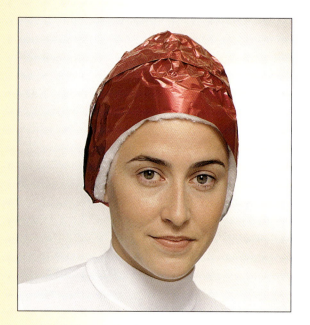

11 Wrap the head in foil and develop the colour with heat for 30–60 minutes. The longer the development time, the more intensive the colour. Rinse thoroughly, shampoo three times, condition and style as normal.

TIPS

- Add a little extra milk if the paste begins to dry out.

- With repeated usage, henna can build up on the hair shaft giving a dull, coated effect. To remove this, mix together a solution of 70% alcohol and 30% mineral oil, apply it from roots to ends and leave for 30 minutes. This will loosen the build-up and enable the residues to be rinsed away. You may need to repeat the process two or three times.

Product used
Natural red henna

SEMI-PERMANENTS

Semi-permanent colours will make hair the same depth as the natural base or darker but will not lighten it. They are most often used to change the tone of the hair by adding gold, red, copper or burgundy hues.

HOW THEY WORK

These formulations work by depositing colour molecules in the hair. The molecules penetrate the cuticle and enter the cortex, where they combine with the hydrogen bonds. In order to do this, the colour molecules need to be relatively small, and the products have a pH of between 8 and 9 to aid this penetration. Each time the hair is shampooed, some of the colour molecules are replaced by water, causing the colour to weaken. By the fifth or sixth time the hair is shampooed, the colour is likely to be completely lost. Semi-permanent colour should be applied to freshly shampooed hair which has been towel-dried to prevent dilution of the product. Development time is 10–30 minutes.

ADVANTAGES

- certain types will effectively cover up to 100% white hair
- good for correcting yellow tones in pre-lightened or white hair
- useful for brightening and enhancing hair colour between permanent tint applications
- no commitment from client, so semis are a good introduction to colour
- adds shine and gloss to the hair
- ideal for creating bold fashion colours
- unlikely to cause scalp irritation and allergy
- may safely be used after a permanent wave

DISADVANTAGES

- wash out within four to six shampoos
- result can be patchy on unevenly porous hair
- cannot lighten hair

LONGER-LASTING SEMI-PERMANENTS

Sometimes called quasi colours, these are non-lightening colourants and are a cross between semis and permanents. They are mixtures of nitro-phenylenediamines and/or anthraquinones (found in semi-permanent colourants) and para-dyes (found in permanents) and need to be combined with an oxidising agent. The semi-permanent part of a cosmetic colourant will gradually wash out of the hair but the loss of colour will not be complete because of the permanence of the para-dyes. Consequently, these colourants will last longer – up to 21 shampoos – and will result in a demarcation line. The strength of hydrogen peroxide added to cosmetic colourants is relatively low, normally between 1% and 3% (6–10 vol.). Manufacturers may call the oxidant a colour developer or activator to emphasise the difference in strength of the oxidant and to avoid using the words hydrogen peroxide, which may be associated with hair damage. This type of colourant should be treated in a similar manner to permanent tint, and a skin test is essential because of the inclusion of the para-dye.

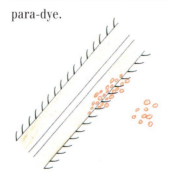

Colour molecules penetrate the cuticle layers and the outer edge of the cortex

HOW TO APPLY A SEMI-PERMANENT

Before

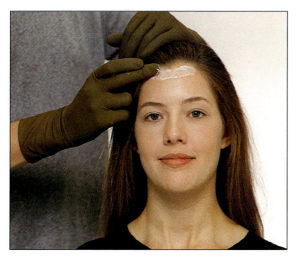

1 Apply barrier cream around the hairline.

2 Using a sponge, apply the colour to the mid-lengths and ends.

3 Start at the nape of the neck and work up towards the crown.

TIP

Wipe the colour away from the tiny hairs on the hairline so this area is not too dark and looks more natural.

4 Completed back sections.

5 Use a brush to apply the colour to the front hairline to ensure it stays neat and clean. Continue with the sponge through the rest of the hair.

6 Once the colour has been applied, massage thoroughly and pile the hair up on top of the head.

7 Re-apply the barrier cream and place a cotton wool strip around the hairline.

8 Cover the hair with a plastic hat and develop the colour naturally, or with heat for a more intensive result. Allow product to develop, then shampoo, condition and style as required.

Products used
Chestnut Brown and Golden Blonde Semi-Permanent, mixed together to give Golden Chestnut Brown

PERMANENT TINT

Permanent colour offers the ultimate service: it can be used to add an infinite variety of shades and gives complete coverage of grey hair. The earliest oxidation or permanent dyes, which produced a brown compound, were made with para-phenylenediamine. They thus became known as para-dyes. Other chemicals are now used to give a wider range of colours. These include para-aminophenol (reddish brown), meta-dihydroxybenzene (grey) and meta-phenylenediamine (brown). Mixtures of these dyes are prepared as thick liquids or creams designed to be mixed with hydrogen peroxide immediately before use.

HOW THEY WORK

These dyes lighten the melanin and tint the hair at the same time. Basically, permanent or oxidation dyes remain ineffective until they are mixed with hydrogen peroxide. Hydrogen peroxide is made up of two atoms of oxygen and two atoms of hydrogen (H_2O_2) and is available in cream or liquid form. Chemists identify the different strengths by %. Cosmetologists identify the strength by volume because it is the freeing of a certain volume of gases that creates the chemical reaction. The different strengths and uses are as follows:

10 vol. (3%)
- tinting dark shades, i.e. black or blue-black
- toners on pre-lightened hair
- covering grey hair
- pre-softening resistant hair
- refreshing a tint

20 vol. (6%)
- all regular colouring
- up to 1 shade of lift

30 vol. (9%)
- 2–3 shades of lift

40 vol. (12%)
- 3–4 shades of lift

If more than four shades of lift are required, then you need to use a high-lift tint which uses double the amount of hydrogen peroxide or has its own developer. If even more lift is required, then lightener (bleach) will be needed. Hydrogen peroxide is sold in 100 vol. strength, which can be diluted down, but there is no need to use anything stronger than 40 vol.

Hydrogen peroxide will only release oxygen molecules when in an alkaline state and this is one reason why all oxidation dye products contain a small amount of ammonia. This returns the hydrogen peroxide to its natural alkaline state and allows it to release its oxygen freely. The ammonia also opens the hair shaft so that the molecules can penetrate the hair during colouring.

Dye molecules enter the hair shaft (which has been opened by the ammonia) along with, but separate from, the molecules of free oxygen. A chemical reaction joins the free oxygen to the uncoloured dye molecules, and both become coloured. They are now so large that they become trapped within the hair shaft.

TRUE COLOURS

With oxidation dyes, true brown shades are available and consequently no off-shades will be encountered as with semi-permanent dyes. The colour is permanent both because the final colour particles are trapped in the hair shaft and additionally because in this state they are insoluble in water.

Colour molecules pass through the cuticle into the cortex

The colour molecules swell and join together, becoming permanently trapped in the hair shaft

PROBLEMS

Colour fade is generally due to the cuticle being raised and damaged, allowing the dyes to wash from the hair. This can be the result of over-processing or unnecessary combing-through of undiluted tint, but it is more often the result of excessive heat styling, sun exposure or chlorine build-up on the hair.

Lack of coverage is generally the result of applying too little colour or not leaving it on long enough, in which case there will be particles of dye which do not bond with oxygen, and so wash away when the colour is removed.

Hair resistant to colour could be caused by closely packed cuticle scales – strong white hairs are often resistant to tint. Pre-softening to open the cuticle scales may be necessary. To do this, run a 10 vol. hydrogen peroxide solution through the hair, leave for 20 minutes, then rinse in cool water before applying the colour.

ADVANTAGES

- permanently changes hair colour
- can lighten and tone hair simultaneously
- 100% coverage of white hair
- durability
- wide choice of shades
- versatility
- softens wiry hair, making it more malleable
- adds texture to the hair

DISADVANTAGES

- requires client commitment – roots need retouching every four to six weeks
- colour fade on damaged hair
- danger of dye dermatitis – always do a skin test prior to application

HOW TO APPLY A LIGHTER TINT

Before

1 Section the hair into four, dividing the hair from the crown to the top of the ears and then from the centre of the forehead to the nape of the neck.

2 Apply barrier cream for protection.

3 Starting at the back of the head, take the first section.

4 Using horizontal sections, apply the colour initially to the mid-lengths and ends only.

5 Use strips of cotton wool to block off the root area.

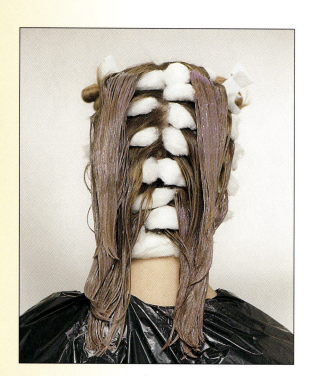

6 Completed colour application from the back.

7 Continue the process through the front, applying the colour to the mid-lengths and ends only.

TIP

Ensure the hair is completely saturated with the product – a thorough application is essential for even results.

8 Take sections vertically through the front and comb them back off the face.

9 Completed colour application from the front.

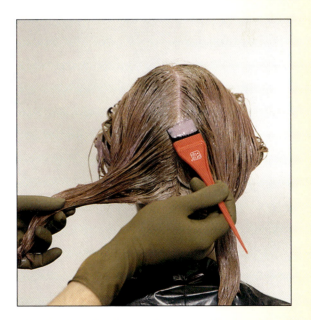

10 Apply the colour to the roots, at approximately half the degree of lift required.

11 Working through the back sections, apply the colour to the roots only.

SAFETY PRECAUTIONS WHEN TINTING

- Always use clean dry bowls and brushes as any residues could affect your end colour result.

- Avoid irritating the scalp by excessive brushing, shampooing or blow-drying the hair before tinting.

- Follow the manufacturer's guidelines, especially on mixing and on development times.

- Always mix in a non-metallic bowl.

- Wear gloves to protect your hands from stains and chemical burns.

Product used

Apricot Blonde Permanent Tint

12 Apply the colour to the roots in diagonal sections.

13 Once the colour has been applied to the roots, mix fresh colour and re-apply to the ends. Allow product to develop, then shampoo, condition and style as required.

HOW TO APPLY A ROOT REGROWTH TINT

Before

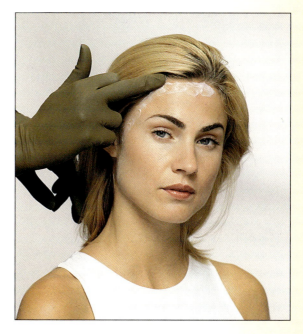

1 Apply barrier cream around the hairline.

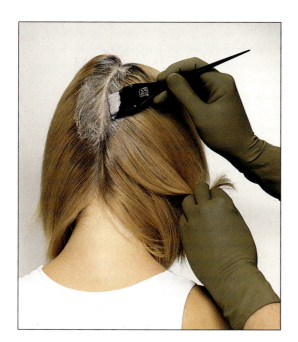

2 Take a section from the crown down to the nape of the neck. Apply the colour to the regrowth area only.

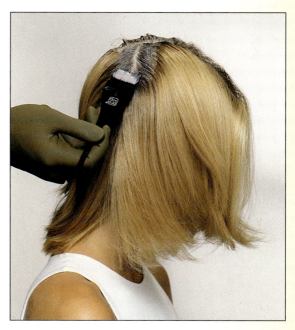

3 Take a further section from the crown to the top of the ear and apply the colour in the same way.

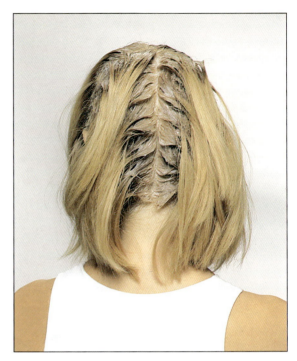

4 Repeat this on the other side. The back of the head is now divided into two sections. Take diagonal sections and apply the colour to the roots only.

5 Completed colour application at the back.

6 Repeat the process through the front sections, applying the colour to the roots only. Ensure the hairline is clean and re-apply the barrier cream. Allow product to develop, then shampoo, condition and style as required.

TIPS

• Take fine sections to ensure the roots are completely covered.

• Double check to make sure no area has been missed.

Product used
Light Golden Blonde Permanent Tint

COLOUR-MATCHING THE ENDS

When a client comes to have her regrowth tinted, you will also have to match the ends of her hair with the colour of the original tint. Depending on the degree of fade on the ends, you can:

- Apply undiluted tint to the ends immediately after the root application or apply just for the last 15 minutes of development time.

- Dilute the same colour as the root application with a little water and apply to the ends.

- Mix fresh tint with equal amounts of shampoo and hydrogen peroxide and apply to the ends – we call this a colour bath.

- Partially emulsify: at the backwash, sprinkle water on the head before massaging colour through to the ends and leave to develop for at least 10–15 minutes.

- Apply a semi-permanent colour after the permanent tint has been washed off.

- Spray the lengths with water and simply comb the tint through.

- Mix one part tint to three parts water and apply to the ends immediately after root application and allow to develop for 30 minutes. Then mix 10 ml of 9% (30 vol.) hydrogen peroxide with 40 ml of warm water and apply to mid-lengths and ends and leave to develop for a further 5 minutes.

How to tone with tint

Before

1 Apply barrier cream around the hairline.

2 Take a section from the crown down to the nape of the neck and apply colour to the roots.

3 Take a further section from the crown to the top of the ear and apply colour to the roots.

4 Take diagonal sections across the back of the head and apply the colour to the roots only.

5 Completed back sections.

6 Take diagonal sections through the front of the head.

7 Regrowth colour application completed.

8 Starting at the nape of the neck, apply the colour to the mid-lengths and ends immediately.

9 Completed application. Allow product to develop, then shampoo, condition and style as required.

TIP

Remember to cross-check root application, i.e. take sections the opposite way to check that no area has been missed.

Product used
Strawberry Blonde Permanent Tint

LIGHTENERS

Hair lighteners come in a variety of guises and are used to remove colour from the hair. Basically they are alkalisers, i.e. products that supply sufficient alkali to destabilise hydrogen peroxide when the two are mixed. The hydrogen peroxide then attacks the pigment in the hair and lightens it. Hydrogen peroxide is stabilised in the bottle at a low pH (typically around 3.0–3.5). When the lightener is added, it brings the mixture to 9.0 or above, triggering the oxygen release.

TYPES OF LIGHTENER

Lighteners are available in two forms: powder and lotion. The latter can be liquid-, oil- or gel-based.

Powder lighteners are generally stronger and faster and are used for off-the-scalp lightening, where the product does not come into contact with the skin or scalp. The lifting ability depends on the strength of the hydrogen peroxide used.

Lotion lighteners generally have a smoother consistency and are formulated to protect the skin and scalp. These can therefore be used for on-the-scalp lightening processes.

INGREDIENTS

The chemicals used in lighteners are ammonia, ammonium hydroxide, ammonium, magnesium silicate and sodium. All lighteners are mixed with hydrogen peroxide before use.

WHEN TO USE

Lighteners are used when hair colourants are not strong enough to achieve the degree of lightening required, i.e. for highlights, pastel blonde effects or when the hair is strongly pigmented and naturally dark in colour.

MIXING

Specific mixing instructions vary according to the product used. Powder lighteners are mixed with hydrogen peroxide to produce a smooth, slightly stiff, creamy mixture. For lotion lighteners, double amounts of hydrogen peroxide are generally used.

Lotion lighteners and booster powders must be mixed in sequence: dissolve booster powders in hydrogen peroxide completely, then add the lotion lightener. If you mix the three components in a different sequence, the booster powder will not dissolve properly, and you will end up with a lumpy mixture. This could cause a patchy or uneven result.

STAGES OF LIGHTENING

When lightening hair with a lightener, it goes through a process known as the seven stages of lift. A lightener has no lifting limitations – it has the ability to remove all colour pigment from the hair.

The stages of lightening are: red-brown, red, orange, gold, yellow-gold, yellow and pale yellow. The deeper the natural base colour, the more stages you must go through to achieve maximum lightness.

ADVANTAGES

- lightens hair
- can be used as a colour corrector
- adds texture

DISADVANTAGES

- regrowth needs retouching regularly
- can irritate the skin
- lightened hair must be protected from strong sunlight, ultra violet light and chlorinated water

Before

WHOLE HEAD LIGHTENING

Dramatic results are achieved with lighteners

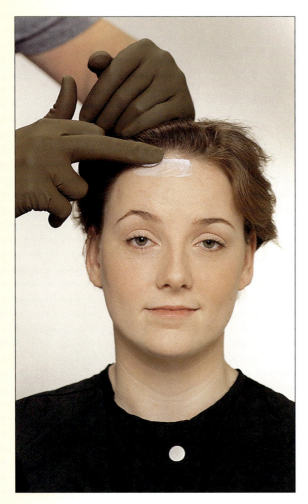

1 Apply barrier cream for protection.

2 Section the hair into four from the crown to the top of the ears and then from the centre of the forehead to the nape of the neck.

TIPS

- Most manufacturers recommend that you do not go beyond a pale yellow base because of the risk of losing all the colour pigment, which would lead to the hair not holding a toner.

- Wear protective gloves.

- Follow mixing instructions precisely.

- Always use a non-metallic bowl for mixing and make sure you are in a well-ventilated area.

3 Starting at the back of the head, take horizontal sections and initially apply lightener to the mid-lengths and ends only.

4 Block off the root area with strips of cotton wool.

49

5 Completed lightener application from the back.

6 Continue the process through the front and sides, applying the lightener to the mid-lengths and ends only.

7 Completed lightener application from the side.

8 Completed lightener application from the top.

9 At approximately half the degree of lift required, remove the cotton wool strips.

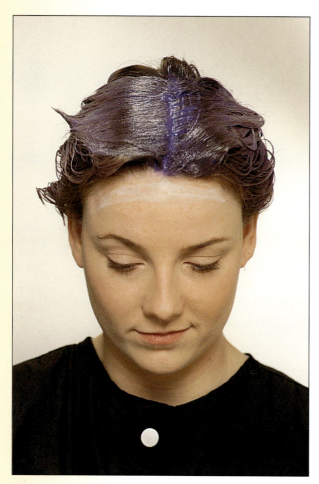

10 Apply lightener to the roots only.

11 Once the lightener has been applied to the roots, fresh lightener is mixed and re-applied to the ends. Product is then left for full development time before rinsing. Shampoo, condition and style as required.

TIP

To ensure an even result, make sure the ends are light enough before applying the colour to the roots.

Product used
Lightener

52

Partial Lightening

Before

1 Section off the sides in V-sections taken from the temple area and working around to the back of the head. Apply barrier cream to the area not to be coloured.

2 Apply a protective layer of foil.

3 Spray the top section with hairspray.

4 Apply heat and work the hair upwards to encourage it to stand up.

5 Apply colour to the mid-lengths and ends.

6 Place cotton wool at the roots as a protection. Work sections backwards, away from the face.

7 Continue working through to the front of the head. Then continue this process on the other side.

8 Completed colour application from the back.

9 Final colour application from the side. Allow product to develop, then shampoo, condition and style as required.

TIP

On the mid-lengths, leave a little more regrowth than you require to allow for colour expansion during the oxidation process.

Product used
Lightener

FOIL TECHNIQUES

The quality of results achieved using foil techniques cannot be matched. Whole head highlights are time-consuming but clients are always thrilled with the result. Foil can also be used for partial hair colouring techniques, giving interesting and effective results.

Before

CLASSIC FOIL HIGHLIGHTS

1 Section off the head into 11 sections. Separate the front and back initially by taking a section from the crown – where the hair breaks, down to the top of the ears. Take a small square in the front, using an equal amount from each side of the parting. Using the natural recession area at the temples, take each side into two sections. This gives five sections on the front of the head.

2 Take a triangular section at the crown.

3 Side view of the front sections.

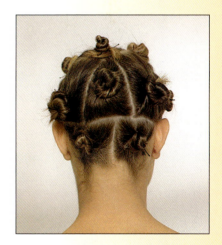

4 Take a section from ear to ear across the occipital bone. Divide the area above this into three vertical sections, and the area underneath into two.

5 Take the first section following the growth pattern of the hairline.

6 Using a pintail comb, weave out highlights.

7 Lay the highlights on the foil, ensuring the foil is right up to the root area.

8 Use a brush to apply the colour. Ensure all the hair is covered.

9 Fold the foil in half...

10 ... and then in half again.

11 Using the end of the pintail comb, fold the foil vertically at each end towards the centre.

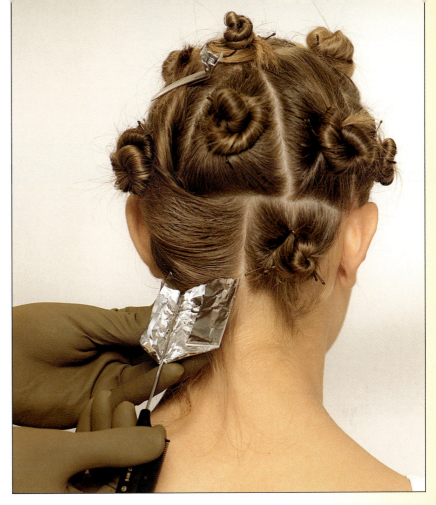

12 Fold a second piece of foil in half...

13 ... and then in half again.

14 Wrap this around the root area – not only to keep the foil firm and in place but also to prevent seepage when the colour oxidises in the foil.

15 Completed highlight package.

16 Take the next section diagonally, following the hairline around the side of the head. This area is important on longer hair, especially if it is to be worn up.

17 Work the next sections vertically. This shows the first two sections completed.

18 Work the remaining back hair in the same way.

19 Steps 18 and 19 show the importance of brick-working the highlights. Make sure that the new section lights fall in between those of the previous section.

20 As the head shape curves towards the crown, combine the adjacent sections.

21 Work the triangular section at the crown horizontally towards the crown.

22 Follow the contour of the hairline as you weave out the highlights. Work the side sections backwards following the same pattern.

23 Follow the contour on the front hairline and then work these sections backwards.

24 The square in front is simply worked backwards. This is so that whichever way the fringe moves – right, left or back – the highlights move with it.

25 Now work the top section upwards toward the parting. Continue the process on the other side.

26 Completed highlights from the front.

27 Side view.

28 Back view. Allow product to develop, then shampoo, condition and style as required.

TIPS

- Ensure that you leave a slight gap at the roots when applying the colour so that when the colour oxidises it does not bleed from the foil.

- When using two or more colours, remember to alternate them.

- Seal your packets carefully to avoid seepage.

- Make sure your weaving is equally spaced and that the strands are of the same thickness.

- Remember to brick-work the highlights.

- Depending on your client's natural colour and the tone of the highlights, it may be possible on subsequent alternate visits to merely apply colour to the hairline, parting and crown areas.

Products used
Lightener; Light Honey
Blonde Permanent Tint

SINGLES

Individual chunky highlights add ripples of colour

Before

1 Section off the head in preparation for colour.

2 Place a single chunky highlight on the foil.

3 Apply the first colour, making sure you get close to the roots.

4 Fold the foil. Continue working back, following the contour of the hairline.

5 Colour a single using the second colour.

6 Fold the foil in half, and then into the centre.

7 Fold in the other side to make a large triangle.

8 Pinch the foil at the root and twist the end to create a fluted effect. Continue working until one side is complete.

9 Work the other side in same manner. Allow product to develop, then shampoo, condition and style as required.

TIPS

- Singles can be used to colour the whole head or to emphasise a certain area of the haircut.

- Make sure the foil is not pulled away from the root when it is twisted.

- When using two or more colours, remember to alternate them.

Products used

Light Ash Blonde, Warm Copper and Light Golden Blonde Permanent Tint

SLICES

Bold circles of light shimmer through the hair

Before

1 Divide the hair into six sections, working with the weight line of the haircut and the way the hair falls naturally.

2 Side view.

3 Top view.

4 Using a pintail comb, take a slice of hair.

5 Place the hair on the foil, ensuring the foil sits flush with the root.

6 Apply the first colour to the hair. Make sure the colour goes down to within 2 mm of the root.

7 Fold the foil and wrap a second foil around the base of the first.

8 Work through the back in diagonal sections.

9 Now work across and up towards the crown.

10 Remember to work the colours through the hair evenly.

11 Follow the contour of the hairline as you work the side sections back diagonally.

12 Follow this pattern through the top sections.

13 Take horizontal sections on the last few sections on the parting.

14 The completed head. Allow product to develop, then shampoo, condition and style as required.

Products used

Lightest Blonde, Medium Golden Blonde and Light Copper Permanent Tint

SPECIALIST TECHNIQUES

Using your basic knowledge about tint and foil applications, it is easy to combine these techniques to produce a variety of colour results that are quick, easy and very effective. When you are being creative with colour, the haircut is your canvas, so you should use your expertise to bring it alive with your choice of colour combinations.

TINT AND SLICES

A technique that allows a double process in one

Before

1 From the parting, take a diagonal section level with the top of the ear.

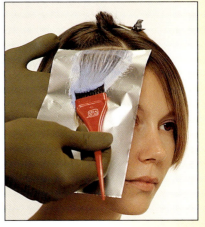

2 Take a fine slice of hair and apply the lightener.

3 Follow this pattern, alternating the lightener with the first colour.

4 Repeat the process on the other side. It is important to keep the angle of placement the same.

TIP

When using a multi-colour application, it is essential to shampoo and rinse hair very thoroughly and quickly to ensure that the colours do not merge together.

5 Work through the top sections, alternating the lightener and the first colour.

6 Completed head.

7 Using a brush, apply the second colour to the rest of the hair.

8 Always work neatly and cleanly, combing colour through ends on longer lengths of hair.

9 Clip the foils up out of the way and leave to process. Allow product to develop, then shampoo, condition and style as required.

TIP

Make sure that when you apply the overall tint you get in between the foils so that the colour blends between the highlights.

Products used

Lightener; Chocolate Brown and Vibrant Red Permanent Tint

CIRCLES

Colour follows the contours of the head for a cascading effect

Before

1 Section the hair into four circles around the head.

2 Apply barrier cream around the hairline.

3 Apply the first colour to the first section from the roots to the ends.

4 Wrap the hair around the head.

TIP

The more circles – i.e. the more sections – the bolder the look. When using vibrant colours, use fewer circles.

5 Place a protective layer of foil over the first section. Apply the second colour to the second section.

6 Place foil on top.

7 Apply the third colour to section three.

8 Finally, apply the second colour to section four. Allow product to develop, then shampoo, condition and style as required.

Products used

Light Caramel Blonde,
Deep Auburn and
Rich Copper Permanent Tint

82

Before

SHADING

Creates shadows that play through the hair

1 Apply barrier cream around the hairline.

2 Apply Belavance Shine Light – a two-stage lightener – to the root area.

3 Take the colour through to the mid-lengths and ends immediately.

4 Completed colour application. Leave to develop for 20 minutes, then shampoo and towel-dry hair.

5 Apply Chestnut Brown Shine & Tone to the root area, leaving the front out.

6 Completed root application.

7 Apply Cherry Red Shine & Tone to the mid-lengths and ends, and finally to the front area.

8 Completed colour, with cotton wool applied. Allow product to develop, shampoo, condition and style as required.

TIP

For best results, always apply the colour to roots first, then to mid-lengths and ends.

Products used

Belavance Color by Labothene International, Pforzheim, Germany: Shine Light is a special two-stage product which will lift the natural base two shades lighter. Shine & Tone – Chestnut Brown and Cherry Red used here – is a semi-permanent colour which has a development time of 10–30 minutes and can be used for natural colour. It is also designed to go over Shine Light.

Duo-tone

A single flash of colour gives instant impact

Before

1 Take a zig-zag section through the front.

2 Apply the first colour and protect with foil.

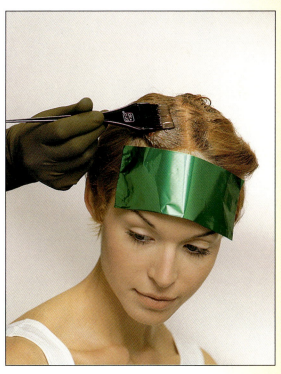

3 Apply the second colour to the rest of the hair, using a brush on the root area.

TIPS

• Ensure sections are perfect before application.

• Always work neatly and cleanly.

4 Complete the application of the second colour direct from the bottle.

Products used

Honey Blonde and
Rich Chocolate Brown
Permanent Tint

5 Completed application. Allow product to develop, then shampoo, condition and style as required.

TIME ZONE

Colour graduates through lengths of hair

Before

1 Section the hair into three.

2 Apply barrier cream to the hairline for protection.

3 Apply Shine Light to the first section. This will lift the hair two shades lighter than the natural colour.

4 Completed colour application on the first section.

5 Place foil over the first section for protection.

6 After 10 minutes, apply Shine Light to the second section.

7 Cover with foil.

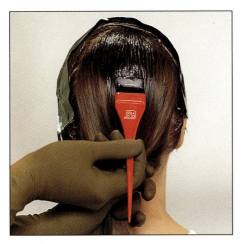

8 After another 10 minutes, colour the back section.

9 Completed colour application.

10 Shows the graduation in colour after the staggered development time – i.e. the front section was developed for 30 minutes, the middle section for 20 minutes and the back section for 10 minutes.

11 Apply Shine & Tone.

12 Complete the application direct from the bottle. Allow product to develop, then shampoo, condition and style as required.

TIP

To be effective you must get your timings exactly right.

Products used

Belavance Color by Labothene International, Pforzheim, Germany: Shine Light; Shine & Tone, Ruby Red

MOSAIC

A chequerboard application gives myriad colour results

Before

1 Starting at the crown, take triangular sections through the whole head.

2 Back of the head sectioned off.

3 Apply the first colour to the whole of the first section, roots to ends.

TIPPING

Emphasise curls by tipping ends with blonde

Before

1 Section off the hair following the natural contours and partings.

2 Completed sections seen from the top of the head.

3 Take a section of hair and weave out chunky highlights.

TIP

Curls tighten as they dry, so make sure you apply colour to at least half an inch of hair.

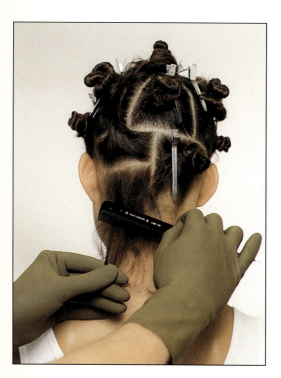

4 Backcomb the highlights so that there will be no line where the lightener stops and starts.

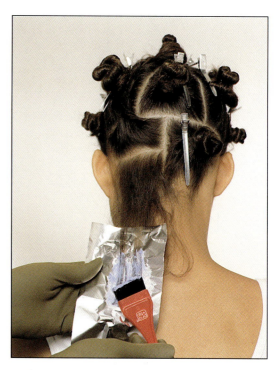

5 Lay the hair on the foil and apply the lightener to the ends only.

6 Fold the foil in half.

7 Then fold in half again.

8 Make a diagonal fold using the pintail comb.

9 Fold the opposite side in, thereby making a triangle.

10 Work up the back of the head to the crown. Here we see the back section completed.

11 Taking diagonal sections, work through the front, always remembering to backcomb before applying lightener.

12 Completed head.

13 Using a brush, apply tint to the rest of the head.

14 Completed colour. Allow product to develop, then shampoo, condition and style as required.

Products used

Lightener; Heather Brown
Permanent Tint

MULTI-COLOUR

A beautiful way to emphasise the lines of a disconnected haircut

Before

1 Working with the longer front section, take a centre parting. From that, take a slice following the contour of the hairline.

2 Apply the first colour to the root area, the lightener to the middle section and the second colour to the ends.

3 Place a second foil over the first to ensure the colours do not bleed. Fold to form a packet. Do another section, this time applying the third and fourth colours and then the lightener.

4 In order to prevent the colour bleeding from the foil, a third foil needs to be placed around the root area, as shown here. To do this, fold the third foil in half, lengthways...

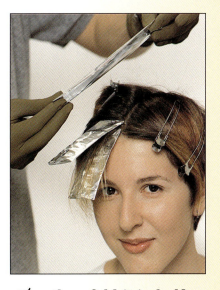

5 ... then fold it in half again, before wrapping it around the root area.

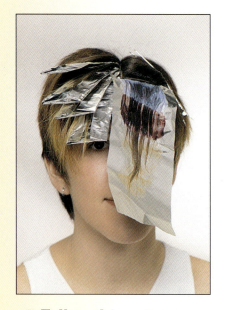

TIP

Make a note of the order of your colour application.

Products used
Lightener; Vibrant Red, Copper Gold, Medium Brown and Lightest Blonde Permanent Tint

6 Follow this pattern on the other side, remembering always to utilise all the colours in a variety of combinations.

7 Front completed.

8 Taking circular sections from the crown, apply the second colour to one section.

9 Section off and clip the rest of the hair. Then apply the lightener and the colours randomly to each of these sections.

10 Clip the foils up so the colour doesn't fall over the client's face. Allow product to develop, then shampoo, condition and style as required.

TIP

When painting the colour on the hair, keep the applications thin and not too close together.

4 Bring down another section of hair and alternate the second and third colours.

5 Completed side view.

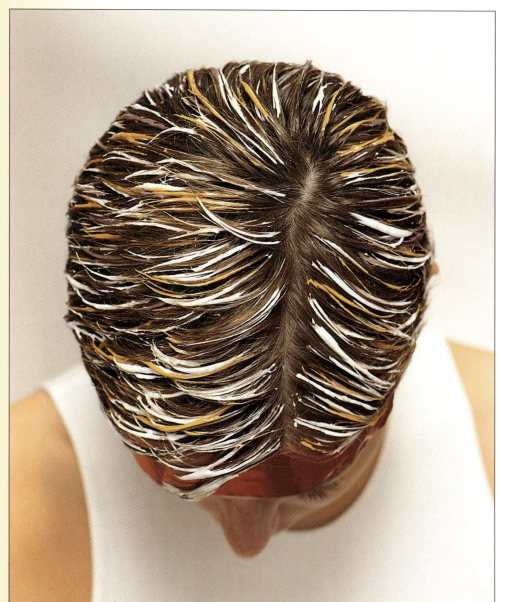

6 Top view. Here we can see the importance of alternating the colours evenly through the hair. Allow full development time for the colour. Then shampoo, condition and style as required.

Products used

Hazel, Copper and Golden Blonde Permanent Tint

POLISHING

A quick and easy application perfect for the ends of short hair

Before

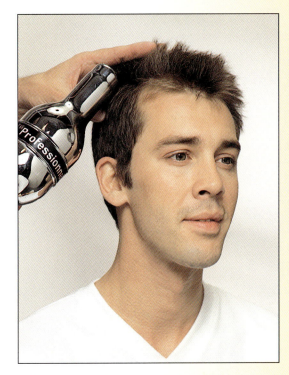

1 Mist the hair with hairspray and apply heat to make the hair stand up.

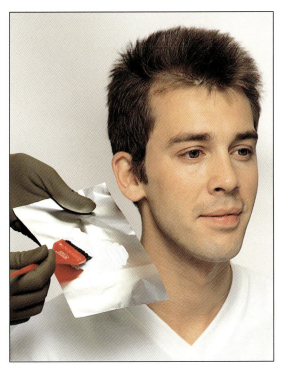

2 Apply the first colour to the foil using a brush.

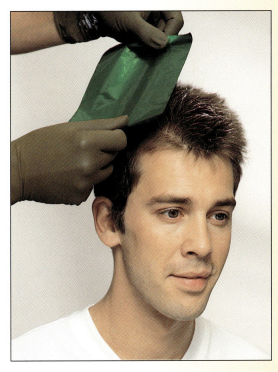

3 Wipe the foil across the surface of the hair to tip the ends with colour.

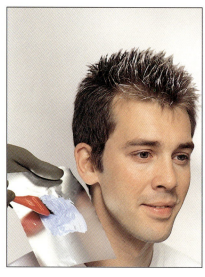

4 Continue in this manner until all the ends are covered.

5 Apply the second colour to the foil.

TIPS

• Be sparing when applying colour, a little goes a long way.

• Don't use too many colours, fewer is better.

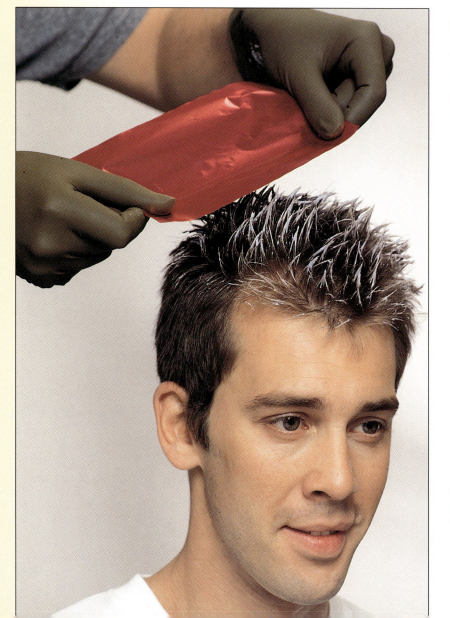

6 Again, wipe the foil across the surface of the hair until the ends are covered as before. Allow product to develop, then shampoo, condition and style as required.

Products used

Light Blonde and Lightest Blonde Lightener

Before

HALO

To emphasise movement around the face

1 Following the contour of the hairline, take a halo section around the head.

2 Back view.

3 Using a brush, apply colour to the whole section.

4 Apply the colour from roots to ends, straight through. Allow product to develop, then shampoo, condition and style as required.

Products used
Light Auburn Permanent Tint

5 Apply the second colour concentrate, icing in between the first colour.

6 Completed colour application.

7 Wipe foil across the head to smudge the colour. Allow product to develop, then shampoo, condition and style as required.

TIPS

- Leave gaps in between the colour concentrates.

- Experiment with and without smudging.

Products used

Light Blonde Permanent Tint; Blue and Violet Concentrate

122

Before

MARBLING

Freehand colouring gives dramatic results

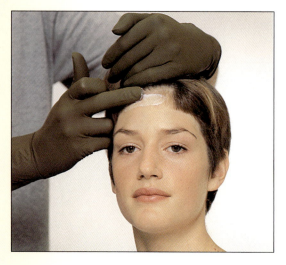

1 Apply barrier cream around the hairline.

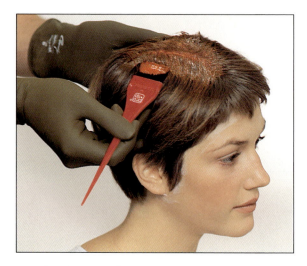

2 Apply the first colour tint to the whole head using a brush.

3 Apply the colour from roots to ends and comb straight through.

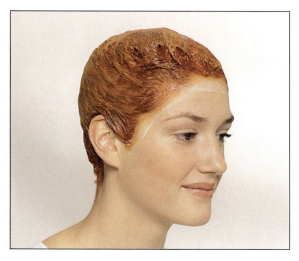

4 Completed colour.

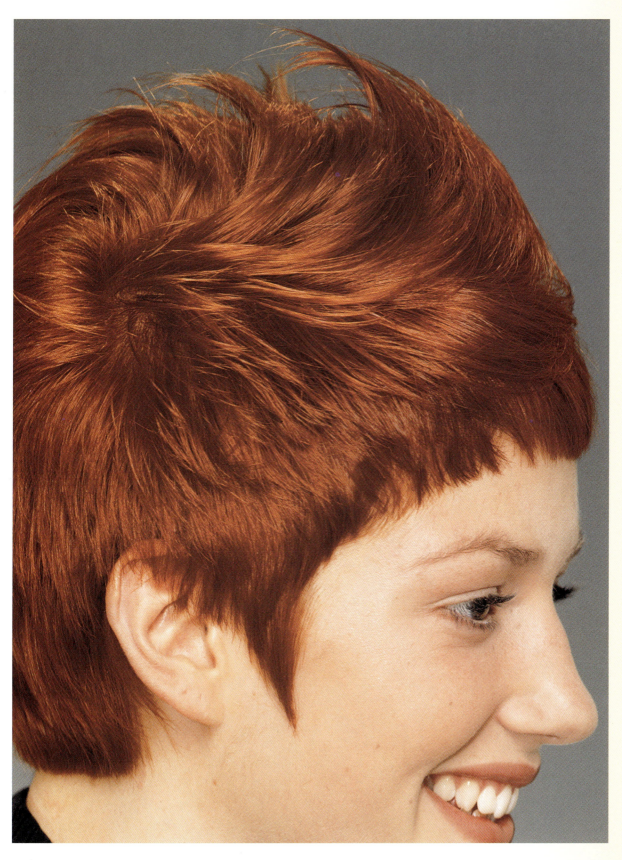

5 Shampoo the hair, condition and dry off.

6 Place a piece of foil across the forehead for protection.

7 Apply the second colour freehand to the tips of the fringe.

8 Place a second piece of foil over the colour so the product does not bleed.

9 Lay the disconnected top section on the foil. Apply the second colour and the lightener freehand in a chequered pattern. Again place a second piece of foil over the top.

10 Marble the other side in a different pattern.

11 Completed application. Allow product to develop, then shampoo, condition and style as required.

Products used

Lightener; Light Copper Red and Dark Brown Permanent Tint

Before

SPONGING

A fun technique to create texture and movement in shorter hair

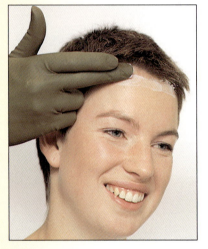

1 Apply barrier cream around the hairline.

2 Apply a pastel blonde tint to the whole head, roots to ends.

3 Shows the tint on the head.

4 Shampoo, condition and dry off.

5 Place a piece of foil
across the forehead
for protection.

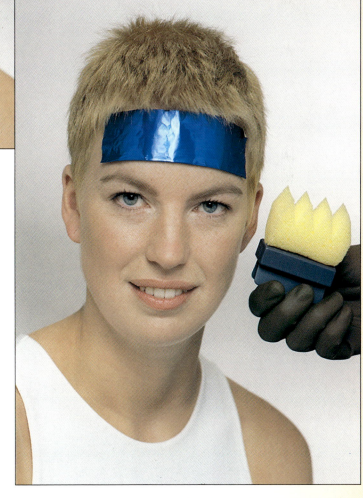

6 Use a sponge to apply the colour.

7 Paint the lightener and the other two colours onto the sponge.

8 Press the sponge onto the head.

9 Apply fresh colour to the sponge in the same order as before and work through the top section.

10 Completed colour. Allow product to develop, then shampoo, condition and style as required.

TIP

Refresh the colour on the sponge before every application but remember less is more with this technique.

Products used

Lightener; Pastel Blonde, Medium Copper and Light Apricot Blonde Permanent Tint

STIPPLING

A high-speed technique perfect for male clients

Before

1 Apply barrier cream to the forehead and then place foil on top.

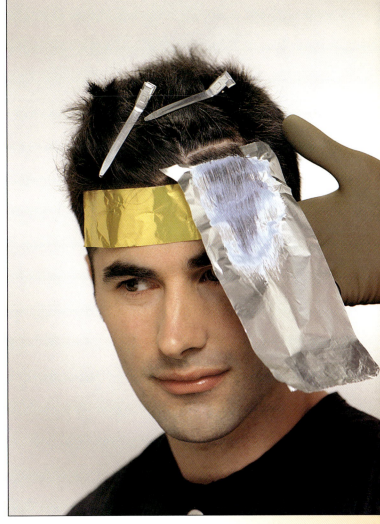

2 Take a slice through the fringe area.

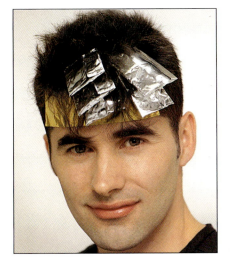

3 Place slices through the longer fringe area. This shows completed fringe area with slices.

4 Apply lightener to a paddle brush.

5 Brush the lightener onto the hair and allow to develop.

6 Shows the colour after the hair has been shampooed. Slicing gives a strong colour effect, brushing a softer effect.

TIP

Do not overdo the brush-on colour.
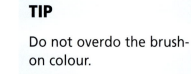

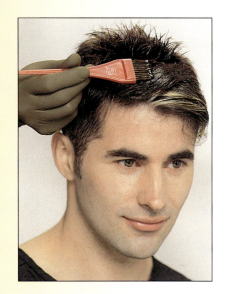

7 Apply Shine & Tone with a brush over the pre-lightened sections.

8 Apply the colour direct from the bottle to the rest of the hair.

9 Completed colour application. Allow product to develop, then shampoo, condition and style as required.

Products used

Lightener; Shine & Tone, Ruby Red

Fantasy colour

Younger clients often want to try vibrant shades that make a real statement about their character and lifestyle. This is when you can let your imagination run riot and mix wondrous shades to create stunning effects.

Before: the hair has been pre-coloured by our model and the result is uneven. However, this will be covered by our application of a semi-permanent conditioning colour.

1 Section the hair from the temple to the top of the ear.

2 Take a slice and paint Apricot onto the root area, then apply Fire to the rest of the section.

3 Reverse the colours on the next section: Fire at the roots and Apricot at the ends.

4 On the next slice use Fire alone. The idea is to apply the colours in random order to achieve a bold result.

5 To ensure that the colours do not run, for each slice place a second piece of foil over the first and then fold.

6 Build up the pattern on the other side. Here Apricot only is applied.

TIP

Do not allow colour to stain the skin and scalp as it can be difficult to remove.

7 Now apply Fire alone to the top section.

8 Apply Tangerine to the back section.

Products used

Tangerine, Fire and Apricot
Crazy Colour

9 Apply Apricot to the side section. This is to create an asymmetric feel for the colour.

10 This shows how the top is Fire, the back and one side Tangerine and the other side Apricot.

COLOUR CORRECTION

Clients who come into the salon for dramatic correction have normally been indulging in a cocktail of home colouring.

Removing or reducing colour can appear complicated and frightening. Consequently many technicians shy away from it, both in training and, more importantly, in the salon. Before you start work on a client's hair you should be confident that its condition will accept the remedy. Remember, once you have started, the result becomes your responsibility.

CONSULTATION

Allow time before the appointment to establish what the client wants to achieve so you can decide on the correction process. Ask what treatments and products have been used over the past year. This will give you an indication of sensitivity and hidden colours.

Your client will expect immediate results, so it might be as well to tactfully remind her that it may take time to achieve the result she wants.

HOW COLOUR REMOVERS WORK

Colour removers are either reducing agents or bleaches. They work by lifting the cuticle and penetrating the hair shaft. Once inside, the remover breaks down the coloured tint molecules, reducing them in size so they are able to escape through the cuticle as the hair is washed.

Often, colour doesn't lift evenly because tints are a mixture of red, brown, yellow and black molecules and the red ones are frequently left behind. Many colour removers are designed to lift out only permanent tint and will not affect natural virgin hair. The strength of product used depends on the density of the colour to be removed and the condition of the hair. Always refer to, and follow, manufacturers' guidelines.

For mild forms of colour build-up, removers are mixed with low-volume hydrogen peroxide, or even water.

PROBLEMS

Colour may not be removed evenly over the entire head because of the varying porosity of the hair. Apply removers to darker areas first, to help even out the end result. Protect virgin regrowth by using a barrier cream or cotton wool to prevent seepage. It may be necessary to repeat the application on darker areas only.

ADVERSE EFFECTS

Lifting the cuticle damages the hair shaft. Such damage must be redressed by conditioning after any colour removal service.

CONTRA-INDICATIONS

Do not colour remove if:
• hair is extremely porous
• skin is broken or sensitive
• you get an adverse reaction to skin or strand test

CHAMELEON EFFECT

While the hair is being treated, it goes through the colour spectrum, including wondrous shades of red, orange and yellow, so remember to warn your client about what to expect and reassure her that the strange colours are only stages in the process.

RE-COLOURING

Once the correct degree of lift is achieved, rinse and shampoo the hair. Then apply a non-barrier-forming conditioner before rinsing and blotting dry.

Remember the client will not be 'back to natural' as the hydrogen peroxide in the original tint will have lightened the natural pigment. What you have is a virgin base on which to apply a different colour. To achieve the required result, more tint will have to be applied.

The regrowth area can be analysed and treated as normal, but you should assess the length for condition, evenness and degree of warm tones before making your colour choice. It may be necessary to re-colour a shade lighter than required as the hair will be extremely porous and will absorb re-applied product very quickly. So the development time will be shorter.

REPEAT PERFORMANCE

Ideally, all colour correction should take place during one appointment – it is not a process that needs to be repeated. However, fine-tuning at a subsequent appointment may be required before optimum results are achieved.

FOLLOW-UP

It is essential that you prescribe and retail the correct shampoo and conditioner for home use. Also, ensure a follow-up appointment is made (not more than two weeks after the initial service) so that the colour can be checked and adjusted if necessary.

AFTER COLOUR CARE

Having invested in a colour service, clients need educating about how to care for and nurture their hair.

THE EFFECTS OF COLOURING

After tinting or colouring, the scalp is often irritated and the natural pH balance is disturbed. The colouring process also causes the hair to swell and the cuticle layers to open, resulting in moisture loss. The inner bonds of the hair themselves have also been disturbed by the oxidation process during colouring. When the tint is rinsed out, there are often stray oxidants left in the hair which, if not neutralised, will continue oxidising and cause the colour to fade.

ENVIRONMENTAL ASSAULTS

Additionally, artificial colour is broken down by oxygen. Every day the oxygen in the air around us is in contact with the hair, slowly causing the colour to fade. Other influences such as strong wind, chlorinated water (which contains high levels of oxygen), salt water and perspiration (which sensitise hair) and sun (which acts as an accelerator) all conspire to speed up the fading process.

PROTECTIVE SHAMPOOS

Shampoos that have a low pH (4.5–5.5) are most suitable for tinted or bleached hair because they help to reduce the oxidation damage and close the cuticle. When the cuticle is closed, the degree of fade, caused by colour molecules escaping, is reduced.

Shampoos designed for after-colour application and home use contain:

- cleansing agents – normally neutral or with an extra-mild action
- anti-oxidants – to neutralise stray oxidants and thereby help prevent fade
- UV filters – to protect the colour from the bleaching properties of the sun
- polymers or moisturising agents – to conserve moisture, smooth cuticles and combat static
- proteins or silicones – to make hair easier to comb, add gloss or sheen; also to add strength, texture and body

SHAMPOOS WITH COLOUR

These are often used on natural and tinted blonde or grey hair. They reduce yellowing and brassiness and revive dull, lack-lustre white hair. The principal ingredient is usually Natural Violet Extract, which counteracts any yellow or brassy colouring. Specialist colour shampoos are also available for use on red, black, brown and auburn hair, and continued use preserves natural-looking tones and keeps the hair looking brighter for longer. The cleansing base is Sodium Laureth Sulfate rather than the harsher Sodium Lauryl Sulphate.

COLOUR MAINTENANCE

Specialist shampoos, and general colour maintenance, should be a natural topic to introduce as an integral part of a colouring service. If you ensure that the appropriate system is to hand – and perhaps offer a care leaflet – then it will be easier to encourage retail sales. Remember, helping your client keep her colour will bring her back into the salon.

TIPS

Clients with coloured hair should be advised to:

- Avoid contact with bright sunlight as much as possible (e.g. wear a hat) – as well as causing fade, it accentuates red tones.

- Rinse salt and chlorinated water from hair immediately after swimming. The chemical reaction between lighteners and copper in the water can give hair a greenish cast.

- Gently towel-dry the hair, rather than rubbing vigorously, after shampooing.

- Use a specialist shampoo as prescribed.

- Use styling products with UV screens.

- Use a conditioner every time they shampoo and have an intensive salon treatment once a month.

GLOSSARY

ammonia a colourless gas composed of hydrogen and nitrogen

base colour the tonal foundation of a specific hair colour

barrier cream protective cream that is resistant against water, alkalis and weak acids; used to protect skin from chemical damage and from staining

bleach a compound that will remove colour pigments from the hair

build-up coatings on the hair shaft

chelating shampoo a deep-cleansing or stripping shampoo that will remove mineral deposits and product build-up from the hair

cortex the inner layer of the hair located between the cuticle and the medulla (the central core of each hair)

cuticle the outer layer of the hair, made up of tiny overlapping scales

depth the lightness or darkness of a specific colour

developer an oxidising agent, usually hydrogen peroxide, which reacts chemically with colouring material to develop colour molecules and create a change in hair colour

emulsify adding water to loosen tint from the scalp and hair; as you add more water and massage the hair, the tint begins to take on the appearance of shampoo

highlights the introduction of lighter colour in small, selected areas to increase overall lightness of hair

hydrogen peroxide an oxidising chemical used to aid the processing of permanent hair colour and lighteners; it can also be referred to as a developer

infusion a liquid made by pouring boiling water over herbs, flowers, leaves or bark, leaving to steep and then straining

lightener bleach

melanin black/brown pigment that determines skin and hair colour

melanocytes cells which produce the pigments melanin and pheomelanin

metallic salts silver, lead or copper sometimes added to henna or used in colour restorers

molecules two or more atoms joined together by a chemical bond

oxidation the process of adding oxygen or removing hydrogen from a substance; chemicals that do this are called oxidising agents or oxidisers

oxygen a tasteless, odourless, gaseous element that makes up 20 per cent of the atmosphere

permanent a penetrating hair dye that enters the cortex of the hair

pH a measurement scale that tells you exactly how acid or alkaline something is

pigment the matter that gives hair its colour

pheomelanin red/yellow pigment in the hair and skin

pre-lightening a service that is given before application of a tint, usually used when lightening hair dramatically

semi-permanent a non-permanent colour that coats and stains the cuticle and the outer layer of the cortex; the colour washes out within four to six shampoos

tone the colour you see, which is a combination of pigments

tint permanent hair colour

titian red or reddish brown